WHAT HUMANS
POSSESS

The Beauty of Humanity

STEPHANIE ST. MARIE

To order additional copies of this book, please contact:
Palibrio
1663 Liberty Drive
Suite 200
Bloomington, IN 47403
Toll Free from the U.S.A 877.407.5847
Toll Free from Mexico 01.800.288.2243
Toll Free from Spain 900.866.949
From other International locations +1.812.671.9757
Fax: 01.812.355.1576
orders@palibrio.com

ISBN: 978-1-5065-5112-8 (sc)
ISBN: 978-1-5065-5113-5 (e)

Library of Congress Control Number: 2023916365

Print information available on the last page

Rev date: 11/22/2023

References

Bible King James

Catechism of the Catholic Church Ascension Edition 2022
Ascension Publishing Group
Westchester, PA

New American Bible NAB
A Saint Joseph Giant Type Edition:
Catholic Book Publishing Co.
New York July 1970

Holy Bible NAB
Catholic Bible Publishers
1989-1990 Edition

Wikipedia

Google

Contents

WHAT HUMANS POSSESS – The Beauty of Humanity

The content of this book is inspirational for the purpose of providing information about our brains, bodies, and our nature. The book is not intended to diagnose or prescribe any one intervention for the reader. Check with your medical doctor for advice on questions or concerns you may have about medical conditions.

Acknowledgements

To God who by sharing his love, wisdom, and grace helped me grasp more deeply the magnificence of our body, mind, and soul the way he designed us.

To my husband who has been my greatest supporter as I ventured into new avenues of learning throughout our marriage.

To my deceased parents who made it possible to receive the private education that taught me about my God while encouraging me to follow what strengths I had and not to worry about the things of the world that others were good at. I desired to help my fellow man in whatever way I could, as they always did.

To my sisters who have always loved me and provided guidance with logical and critical reviews of my attempts to get through life.

To my mentors and teachers who introduced me to areas of the body's neurological and motor systems throughout my academic schooling that fed my interest in knowing what was known about the body to date.

To Kevin McGrew, PhD. Statistician, who confirmed during an hour-long conversation with me, the validity of the new information I was becoming enlightened about through my own hands-on practice experiences working with clients of a wide range of medical conditions of all ages, newborns to older adults with new technology in the late 1990s.

To the deceased Jim Cassily who worked with children on the Autism Spectrum teaching them piano and training them on the Interactive Metronome he developed to help them with timing.

To the deceased Dr. Stanley Greenspan at George Washington University, who specialized in brain studies, found that there was evidence of positive changes happening with these same children receiving the training from Mr. Cassily. I met both gentlemen at a conference.

To all my clients who trusted and shared their stories with me respecting their wholeness of body, mind, and spirituality during the brief times God gave us to journey together.

To my profession based on the philosophy that besides the body and mind, we also have a spiritual element that functions and can influence the healing process from the impact of losses due to developmental delay, diseases, sudden injury, and deficits that unfold in the process of an aging body.

Lastly, to Elena Quevedo who encouraged me to begin writing books having experienced the gifts that God has given me, has prayed for me and my family, and is feeding children all over the world with the FOOD that is eatable and the FOOD that is everlasting.

Introduction

Over the decades of being a career therapist, my focus has been on the body, the brain, and how they work together as a whole. Attending higher education was a faint dream from my youth but I struggled with basic academics my whole life. While attending the University I learned that it was not likely that we could alter a child's learning disability after the age of five, and later the age range expanded to seven, and later the age range extended to nine years where one could hope to impact the brain development deficits. I also learned that from a brain injury like a stroke, where the individual had skills and lost them, these persons could continue to make progress over a period of recovery up to one year. Research studies and anecdotal evidence have changed giving way to new outcomes in healthcare.

My quest was to always work at making a difference in how someone's deficit could improve. I had the opportunity to work with a 9-year-old child in a school setting with the severe effects of Cerebral Palsy from birth. He was in a first-grade classroom for children with a variety of learning challenges. This child was assigned to me as part of my later curriculum before graduation. He was immobile, lying on the floor outside of his semi reclining wheelchair. I observed him in class for a half day to see for myself what skills he had. During that morning's academic programing, the child was addressed like this, "Your name is Tim, Tim is your name." There was nothing in his hands and the activities taking place in the front of the room were outside his visual field from the floor. He was not helped to move into different positions as often as I was wiggling around in my chair. What could I do to tap into his intelligence? There were no books to read that would guide me through a process, so everything was a lesson in my own creativity and discovery.

While thinking about parts of the body, the vision, the touch, the motor skills that I wanted to test for, I had an idea to try individually laminated pictures of hands, mittens, a head, a hat, a sock, a foot, a body, and a jacket. These were familiar items he encountered every day during this wintertime of the year.

When I arrived in class the next day, the boy was in his wheelchair, and we were able to go to a quiet room. This was perfect for us to get to know each other. I looked in his eyes to see if he could look back at me, and he did. I reached out to his hands, and he barely moved his index finger to touch me. Cha… ching!!! this task I had envisioned would work. I verbally instructed this student to touch the clothing picture that was a match with the body part. He touched the picture of the hands first and then the mittens. Next, he selected the shoe and then the foot. Next, he picked the coat and the body. The last set he touched was the head and the hat. Bingo… I was able to tell the teachers and my instructor about the success of this activity so that they could add this method of teaching this child to the child's method of learning and his ability to respond in this academic environment with extremely limited physical and verbal skills.

I knew then that I had to finish this degree and get into the field. Thank you, Lord, for providing me with the inspiration to lead me toward the beautiful fully human being that lay before me in the first-grade classroom that first day of a clinical experience.

That moment gave me insight into the hidden skills of the brain not yet discovered by the academic world, the school, nor the teachers, including my university teacher who was the therapist at this school for years.

Thus, the journey of a lifetime career for me began to unfold. God was actively in my heart, my mind, and in my soul.

CHAPTER ONE

Spirituality

. . . .

The most sacred part of being Human is our Spirituality. We each have a Spiritual nature. "We are less like chimpanzees and more like God's Angels," according to a teaching I heard this morning where Fr. Mike Schmitz from the Hallow podcast mentioned an article by a renowned Angel expert, Fr. Serge-Thomas Bonino, March 2020 EWTN Great Britain.

The action of our Creator imparting to us a portion of His Spiritual nature as a loving gift was given to all of us at conception. You don't have to believe this to have received your Soul.

Our Spirits came from Heaven where they lived before they arrived in our bodies because God existed before time and space.

Conception has only become controversial in these days of relativism; however, it has not been a secret going back to the Primeval History section of the Book of Genesis in the Bible.

CHAPTER 1

First Story of Creation. *In the beginning, when God created the heavens and the earth, the earth was a formless, wasteland, and darkness covered the abyss, while a mighty wind swept over the waters.*

Then God said, "Let there be light." and there was light. God saw how good the light was. God then separated the light from the darkness. God called the light "day", and the darkness he called "night." Thus evening came, and morning followed – the first day.

Then God said, "Let there be a dome in the middle of the waters, to separate one body of water from the other." And so it happened: God made the dome, and it separated the water above the dome from the water below it. God called the dome "the sky." Evening came, and morning followed-the second day.

Then God said, "Let the water under the sky be gathered into a single basin, so that the dry land may appear." And so it happened: the water under the sky was gathered into its basin, and the dry land appeared. God called the dry land "the earth," and the basin of the water he called "the sea." God saw how good it was. Then God said, "Let the earth bring forth vegetation: every kind of plant that bears seed and every kind of fruit tree on earth that bears fruit with its seed in it." And so it happened: the earth brought forth every kind of fruit tree on earth that bears fruit with its seed in it. God saw how good it was . Evening came, and morning followed – the third day.

Then God said, "Let there be lights in the dome of the sky, to separate day from night. Let them mark the fixed times, the days and the years, and serve as luminaries in the dome of the sky, to shed light upon the earth." And so it happened: God made the two great lights, the greater one to govern the day, and the lesser one to govern the night; and he made the stars. God set them in the dome of the sky to shed light upon the earth, to govern the day and the night, and to separate the light from the darkness. God saw how good it was. Evening came, and morning followed – the fourth day.

Then God said, "Let the water teem with an abundance of living creatures, and on the earth let birds fly beneath the dome of the sky." And so it happened: God created the great sea monsters and all kinds of swimming creatures with which the water teems, and all kinds of winged birds. God saw how good it was, and God blessed them, saying, "Be fertile, multiply, and fill the water of the seas: and let the birds multiply on the earth." Evening came, and morning followed – the fifth day.

Then God said, "Let the earth bring forth all kinds of living creatures: cattle, creeping things, and wild animals of all kinds." And so it happened. God made all kinds of wild animals, all kinds of cattle, and all kinds of creeping things of the earth. God saw how good it was.

Then God said: "Let us make man in our image, after our likeness. Let them have dominion over the fish of the sea, the birds of the air, and the cattle, and over all the wild animals and all the creatures that crawl on the ground."

God created man in his image; in the divine image he created him; male and female he created them. God blessed them, saying: "Be fertile and multiply; fill the earth and subdue it." God said, "See, I gave you every seed-bearing plant, all over the earth and every tree that has seed-bearing fruit on it to be your food; and to all the animals of the land, all the birds of the air, and all the living creatures that crawl on the ground, I give all the green plants for food." And so it happened, God looked at everything he had made, and he found it very good. Evening came, and morning followed – the sixth day." Genesis 1: 1-31.

A passage from in the New Testament from the letter of John, an Apostle of Jesus Christ describes the way we receive our Spiritual power.

CHAPTER 1

"In the beginning was the Word, and the Word was with God, and the Word was God. He was in the beginning with God. All things came to be through him, and without him nothing came to be. What came to be through him was life, and this life was the light of the human race; the light shines in the darkness, and the darkness has not overcome it. A man named John [the Baptist] was sent from God. He came for testimony to testify to the light, so that all might believe through him. He was not the light, but came to testify to the light. The true light, which enlightens everyone, was coming into the world. He was in the world, and the world came to be through him, but the world did not know him. He came to what was his own, but his own people did not accept him. But to those who did accept him he gave power to become children of God, to those who believe in his name, who were born not by natural generation nor by human chance nor by a man's decision but of God. And the Word became flesh and made his dwelling among us, and we saw his glory, the glory as of the Father's only Son, full of grace and truth." John 1:1-13

Thus, what Humans possess is everything God blessed us with.

We received body, mind, and a spiritual soul to communicate with our Creator. He gave us the ability to see, hear, smell, touch, and think all the time possessing the gift of a free will to follow and serve our Maker. Humans also received permission and a command from the Creator to rest from the hustling and bustling of life.

Our Spirits were made to seek our Creator and to worship Him. It's no wonder that God's enemy has been trying to lead us away from our connection with our Creator since the beginning of time.

Spirituality is where supernatural gifts operate, where our conscience is formed, where meditation and prayer operate.

The simplest way I found to describe how Humans' spiritualty operates is found in the famous children's Disney movie and book Pinocchio. February 1940. In this story the wooden puppet boy named Pinocchio, is led astray from the carpenter's workshop and down to the circus by an evil character. All the while, his friend Jiminy Cricket (symbolic of his active voice of reason) is attempting to redirect Pinocchio back home to the sculptor who fashioned him named Geppetto. It isn't until Pinocchio runs into the ruins of evil and fear that he realizes how much Geppetto loves him and wants him to come home, that he becomes fully human. The fairy in the story represents the Holy Spirit who gives him life. Geppetto represents God the Father and Creator, and Jiminy Cricket is his guide helping Pinocchio's mind to make better choices.

Humans are living beings with souls gifted to us by God and our Spirituality is the part of us capable of talking with God. We have a place in this created world, and we are here at this moment in time living out our purpose already written about in the Book of Life with our names in it kept for us in Heaven.

How will you finish the final chapter of your book with your name on it in Heaven?

Seek to know the Creator of all living things and cherish each moment of your life in remaining in God's Grace that will help us face the hardships, knowing we can never be separated from His divine Love. If we choose to separate ourselves from Him, then it is our own pride and failure to recognize our own identity, beings created by God for His purpose. The Catechism of the Catholic Church verse 229 teaches us, "Faith in God leads us to turn to him alone as our first origin and our ultimate goal, and neither to prefer anything to him nor to substitute anything for him."

Live now so you can die happily bearing challenges and adversities and sickness. Live virtuously and you will inherit Eternity when you return to your home in Heaven.

Talking with God is a connection He made with us. Our return response is as simple as just spending quiet time being you. Just by being open to His presence you are receiving immeasurable grace. He wants to be part of every moment of our life to guide the vast number of decisions we make throughout each day. Spend time listening to His voice. He is calling each one of us. He is waiting for us to stop what we are doing in order to spend time developing a relationship. He is our Spiritual director, the best lover anyone will ever know in this lifetime. We can count on Him to never leave us. Being Spiritual beings comes with grace, peace, joy, happiness, along with hardships and trials. God is good, and not part of hardship. He is aware of the hardships we go through as part of our journey; however He is LOVE, LIGHT, GOODNESS, and MERCY. He has no evil, does no evil, wishes no evil, never created the evil we live with as Humans. He gave us a way out of the madness. He gave us our Spirituality to rise above what the world offers. He will never let go of your hand. Nothing can separate us from His LOVE.

I prayed to see His face and then a friend told me about The Chosen series of episodes now into their 4th season of production. The story is clearly about Biblical events from the Bible. The character looked like Jesus from paintings and statues of him throughout the ages.

Now my spiritual life is easier having a human representation of the man that played his role in the series. During this time of seeking the face of Jesus, I saw a painter whose painting depicts a similar face that looks like the actor as well. I ordered the picture by the artist found online at gregolsen.com

Another resource I found very moving is "Jesus Calling" book by Sarah Young. Each page is like a love letter from Jesus to the reader. Each reading is based on Old and New Testiment verses gathered into a theme each day to address our Humanity and Spirituality.

Turn on spiritual music. I enjoy music by Elevation Worship just ask Alexa! Attend a prayer meeting. Watch an uplifting movie.

Attending Mass and receiving the Sacraments is a powerful way to refresh our souls. We benefit spiritually more than we can ever see in our Human state but knowing who we are receiving from, the most trustworthy Divine being that ever existed should find us running to Him wherever we can.

Spend time with God speaking to Him and listening for His voice.

CHAPTER T W O

Sleep Deprivation

Over the years of evaluating people with stress, anxiety, and brain injuries I kept hearing about one condition that was interfering with functional daily living reported during initial intake interviews from many of my clients.

Healthy sleep with Circadian Rhythm patterns is getting 8-10 hours of sleep each night without disturbed sleep and reaching a deep theta wave level where the brain can detox back to a healthy state of functioning when it is time to wake up.

Sleep deprivation is a chronic medical condition of the loss of necessary deep brain recovery sleep or poor-quality patterns of sleep where a person has difficulty falling asleep, wakes up during the night, can't fall back to sleep, and experiences fatigue. Waking up as if they had not slept all during the night is a signal of poor-quality brain recovery sleep. This condition of interrupted sleep for 5 hours or less night after night, week after week, month after month, and year after year is a chronic deteriorating health issue and has even been associated with health conditions even to death. This abnormal pattern of sleep deprivation leads to chronic interference with a person's daily productivity.

A sleep deprived individual can have one or more of the following problems - a hard time with self-regulation, night terrors, post-traumatic stress disorder, inability to concentrate, staying awake the next day, and focusing-over-time. A major concern is that this condition over time can lead to trouble completing tasks affecting work productivity. Sleep deprivation can negatively impact the ability to sustain meaningful relationships, no matter who a person is relating to, whether the other person is a parent, spouse, child, boss, coworker, or even if they own their own business having to deal with employees.

Sleep deprivation over a long period of time can lead to medical health conditions and can even be fatal to a person if they don't get the help they need in the early stages.

Quick check questionnaire

1. Do you have trouble falling asleep?

2. Are you able to stay asleep for 6-8 hours?

3. If you wake up during the night to use the bathroom, are you able to fall asleep again relatively quickly?

4. Do you have night terrors during your sleep?

5. Do you wake up with fatigue?

If the answers you selected are YES to more than two of them, then you should speak with your doctor or try some of the things I use to help people in my practice.

THERAPEUTIC INTERVENTIONS FOR SLEEP DEPRIVATION

Over the past 20 years, I have found some amazing therapeutic interventions that helped multiple of my clients of varying ages with a wide range of mental and/or physical conditions.

Sleep deprivation is considered a patterned condition when the individual is not getting enough brain recovery-level quality sleep and wakes up fatigued frequently over a long period of time.

Many clients report having trouble falling asleep, staying asleep, waking up during the night from pain, anxiety, or episodes of night terrors. Even something as normal as waking up to use the bathroom and then not being able to fall asleep happens frequently as reported by my clients. Frequent dream states plague the efforts to get a good night's sleep for many especially when they experience patterns of anxiety, high stress levels, high pain levels, or post-traumatic stress disorder (PTSD) all factors that can impact their sleep patterns.

Three interventions that treat sleep deprivation to override sleep problems.

- Manual therapy to calm nerves and to address areas of trauma and pain.

- Breathing exercises to get more oxygen to the body and brain.

- Sensory integration sound therapy

MANUAL THERAPY - CRANIOSACRAL THERAPY

One of the techniques I use to help someone with sleep deprivation is a manual technique I learned in multiple 5-day Upledger CranioSacral classes. It is called CranioSacral therapy which is a good place to begin for multiple conditions especially for the first-time assessment of the Cranial rhythm. Other Upledger courses "Somato Emotional I and II," techniques address tissue trauma and cell memory that can interfere with sleep linked to anxiety and PTSD.

Resources for the Upledger Institute can be found on their website where you can read case studies on the topic. www.upledgerinstitute.com

I have used other manual therapy techniques to promote sleep and relaxation when I apply a slow gentle stretch that elongates contracted muscles to release trapped toxins and to calm muscle tension that triggers a high alert sympathetic nervous system.

Some chronic pain responds to icing that can dull or block the pain signal to the brain.

Another treatment is a hot pack applied to a painful area that helps to relax tissue when an area needs more circulation and results in soothing relief.

If these home remedies are not helpful to lessen symptoms, then contact your doctor.

DEEP BREATHING EXERCISES

Breathing oxygen deeply into the abdominal area where the lower lobes of the lungs extend is a way of healing. Breathing through the nose with the mouth closed and holding the breath for 5-7 seconds before blowing it out slowly through pierced lips, helps a body to receive more oxygen. During this exercise and as the chest expands outwardly, holding the breath opens the structures of the spine and rib cage so oxygen can get to all parts of the body.

Often when people are sitting for long periods of time at a computer, it is easy to slow down one's breathing resulting in depriving the brain and body of oxygen needed for the brain to function. Straightening one's posture before beginning breathing exercises can be done each hour to get into the habit of the exercise. Taking 4-6 breaths as described above has helped other health conditions to improve simply by engaging, taking initiative, being motivated to heal, and to better your own health through discipline.

SENSORY INTEGRATION SOUND THERAPY

Over a decade ago I was introduced to Dr. Ron Minson and his wife Kate Minson who offered an advanced training session for practitioners from a variety of disciplines. They taught us about new technology developed by sound engineers who understood the benefits of sensory integration and sound.

As an advanced trained and experienced practitioner, I have been using the iLs system found in the Total Focus unit in my practice as well as the DreamPad pillow that both use the same speaker sound system. These devices use a vibrating speaker that subtly yet powerfully helps to calm and balance the sympathetic/parasympathetic nervous systems of the brain, emotions, and sensory systems.

I explain to my clients that the benefit of using this special sound therapy is like taking an "ON/OFF" switch to the brain and restoring it back to "DIMMER SWITCH" functional levels. This provides more alert level options for the brain to select from resulting in brain flexibility. This is essential for transitioning from a state of high alert that is typical following trauma moving gently to a deep state of brain recovery level sleep. The secret sauce is in the vibrating speakers that break into the high alert state by unlocking the prisoner of anxiety, PTSD, or night terrors which comes with a high state of alarm from past traumatic experiences. The benefits can impact the need for medication or supplements.

Once trained and experienced in these advanced therapeutic techniques, I was able to offer these researched sound treatments to the variety of clients I worked with for over two decades now. I found that the outcomes of using these tools benefit my clients greatly. These improvements were new for me to observe and of great interest after hearing about how they had helped people of any age from infants to older adults. I offered these interventions and tried them on myself and my family with good results. I began using these techniques in my pediatric practice, with the elderly in nursing homes, and when visiting individuals in their home settings.

When a baby with colic calmed down for the first time to finally nurse, to the agitated elderly client with dementia becoming more lucid to be able to engage in play returning.

A bouncing ball to me and later, falling into a restful sleep really got my attention and the attention of the facility staff who knew the person's typical temperament. It was evident to me that helping over 90% of the cases I was treating, with calming soothing interventions could positively impact a person's sleep and overall wellbeing was very exciting. The ability to calm an individual down with a portable tool was amazing from a therapist's perspective. Witnessing a person's brain processing systems simply by improving their ability to sleep longer and deeper seemed so powerful. It felt like I was watching a blessing upon the person to be able to help with sleep and brain recovery so vital to a person's functional health, daily participation in life skills, and even their survival that I was hopeful and so were my clients. Finding hope is vital to successful therapy and recovery from any health problem.

You know something is working when you begin to feel energy when you wake up from a deep uninterrupted night's sleep. This is evidence that the brain is reaching the third phase of rapid eye movement sleep and getting to theta wave levels. The brain can detox at this deep sleep level and shut down other functions to focus on recovery from an injured brain to getting rid of anxiety and fear, stop rerunning bad memories, and adjusting chemicals that are out of balance. Restoring the Circadian rhythm is the ultimate state of recovery from the condition of sleep deprivation. A person's health will improve, and the brain will function with better emotional and mental processing speeds with efficiency and clarity.

CHAPTER THREE

Pain

· ·

It has always been confusing to me as to why we use smiley faces to describe pain when we go to the doctor or are in a rehab program and when we are hospitalized. To me, smiley faces measure emotions rather than pain.

Pain is something that a person carries around day and night either from an injury or from part of a body's structure that deteriorates over time. Some pain can be treated best by medication when things are acute and can be discontinued when the body takes over and can heal the injury.

The clients that I see these days are coming to me with traumatic head injuries. When I interview them, I ask them all sorts of questions about daily life skills from sleeping to what they spend their time doing throughout the day. Significant pain becomes problematic when it keeps an individual from being able to do tasks safely or confidently on their own requiring assistance from someone else.

Pain can be measured through levels of functionality and confidence level when performing a daily task. I find it useful to use a (0-10) scale.

0   = "No pain"

1   = "I have to really think about it"

2   = "I have to think about it"

3   = "The pain is talking to me."

4   = "It hurts, and I need something."

           (i.e., medication, a nap, a hot or cold pack on the area)

5   = " I can't pick up a gallon of milk." (8 lbs.)

5-6   = " I can't pick up a half gallon of milk." (4 lbs.)

6   = "I can't hold a pen to write with."

7   = "My back hurts so much that I can't bend over to put on my socks and shoes."

8   = "It hurts too much to be touched, I can't put clothing on over this area."

9   = "I feel nauseous and am about to pass out"

10   = "Call 911"

The pain I treat is mainly chronic pain someone has been struggling with from the time of their traumatic injury that happened at work, or that occurred from some kind of accident with a moving vehicle like a bicycle, a motorcycle, a truck, train, another vehicle, or a pedestrian in the wrong place at the wrong time.

My therapies to address pain include manual therapies, hot/cold packs, massage, CranioSacral therapy, and integration sound therapy to help relax the individual.

Once sleep deprivation and pain are addressed, the person is on a safer path of recovery and restoration of their body, mental health, and functional capacity. My long-term goal or a person is to make a lasting difference in someone's quality of life overall but especially within each one-hour session, I like seeing a smile on someone's face again reporting more energy, less stress, and less pain to get on with their day.

CHAPTER FOUR

Vision

The visual system involves our eyes and the information it brings to the brain. When testing vision, there are things that can go wrong especially during developmental stages from genetic conditions to injuries that happen to the eyes during some kind of accident.

A person may have suffered a head injury that imbalances in one or both eyes, or in one or both brain hemispheres. In these cases, things do not line up when looking at the world. The steps or the edge of a rug, a curb or a door's threshold, the lines on a paper where you need to sign, and to read a book are all messed up. Driving a car with vision dysfunction is not safe until the deficits are corrected by a professional eye specialist or a vision therapist. The injury can result in double vision, trouble stabilizing an object, or measuring space beyond the body. When the eyes stop working together, this incapacitates and individual and they surely need to see a traumatic vision specialist. A person can be helped with special glasses called prism glasses to level out the brain's sense of a stable horizon. This stabilizes the world in front of them to a major extent.

In my practice, working with someone who suffered an injury involving the eyes, I have been able to adjust the sphenoid bone inside the brain to shift the position of some of the misplaced eye components leading to the muscles of the eyes that shifted during the impact of the brain injury with this CranioSacral technique I learned years ago. I have also seen this technique used to partially correct Duane's Syndrome from birth in a 50-year-old individual that had affected his reading comprehension his whole life. These kinds of changes have not ever shown up in any text or medical book because science is just beginning to discover, study, and try new manual therapies.

Through my training and having the confidence with God's help to address some of these delicate brain conditions and specifically, eye function, has been a real game changer for some of my client's and their ability to return to a more restored lifestyle with confidence.

CHAPTER FIVE

Sensory Processing

. . . .

"Oh, it's just a bug" …smack. "Got it." This is part of our sensory processing system.

The leg sensed the light touch of the bug landing on your leg before your brain recognized the signal and your hand reacted swiftly to the spot to intervene. The eyes followed to check out the results of your smack. The location was right on and brushed the bug to send away the remains. A worse scenario… If you missed the bee sound swarming around you, then you will not miss the sting and the immediate pain through the pain sensing system going from the stinger to your spinal cord and going into a fear, fight, or flight defensive mode. I think my response to running has calmed down, getting older and less afraid of bees than when I got stung on the playground at school in third grade.

The sensory system includes all senses that help the brain gather information from the environment around you and within you to process your thoughts and responses whether verbal or non-verbal.

Senses include seeing, hearing, taste, touch, and smell. All are God's gifts to humanity.

In nature, humanity, and the fallen world, not all senses develop or remain intact throughout our lifetimes. The deficit of any of these senses is part of a person's own journey through life with unique trials that come with the loss or deficit or never having had one or more of these senses. Some losses only enhance other senses to become more heightened allowing a person to adjust to and live life at a different level of awareness and with different experiences. Lately, with the airing of shows on television like The Voice and America's Got Talent, we have been able to watch individuals missing some senses, blow our minds with a developed skill where their talent rose beyond our expectations blow through an audition outperforming others with complete sets of intact senses.

Observing these talented performers supports the position the healthcare and society no longer labels individuals as handicapped. Never underestimate the power of humanity to adjust to their skills and the environment.

God made us in his image and likeness. He knows all, sees all, hears all, feels all, and manages all in the physical and Spiritual worlds. He is available to each one of us who He created to get us through life's challenges until we join him in the Glory of Heaven. We have all heard "No man is an island…." We need each other to get through this time on earth as resourceful human beings with a Spiritual Father who loves us and is waiting for our attention and requests to help us no matter how big or small our need is.

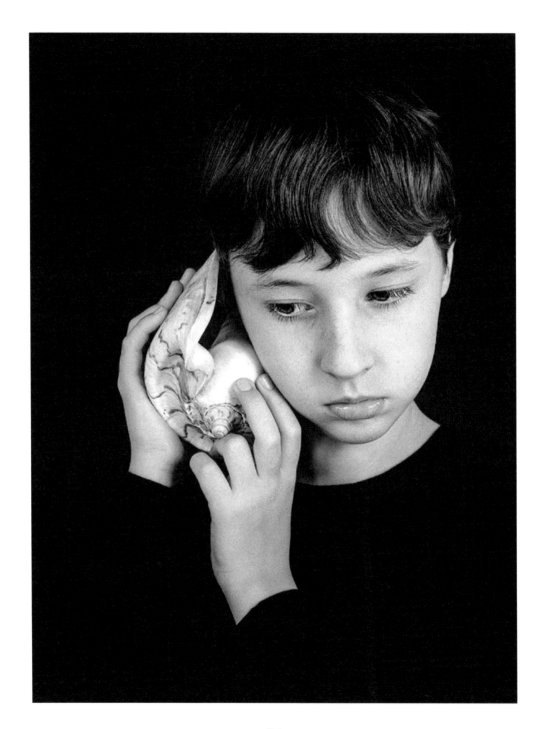

CHAPTER SIX

Auditory Processing

. . . .

"Wa…wa…wa…wa," representing a teacher's voice from the Charlie Brown show

is not that far off from how deficits in auditory processing affect language and comprehension of language. This auditory processing deficit, not hearing the beginning or ending sounds of words, a complex sound environment typical of most classrooms, makes learning stressful and exceedingly difficult for a person who cannot hear distinct sounds for example "f," "sh," "th," "s," "r."

I became enlightened during advanced training in the iLs training program, and it is another tool in my tool pouch when treating auditory processing. A person should check with an Audiology specialist to determine what the state of someone's hearing is to identify the loss of hearing if it exists from nerve damage. If there is no nerve damage in the middle ear, then I can use the iLs devices in my therapy sessions to check for a person hearing filtered music at low Hz levels to 7,000 Hz levels to help the brain lay down a foundation of sound necessary for hearing and speaking language.

One cannot speak what one cannot hear. One cannot spell what one cannot hear. One cannot use the word in a sentence if one cannot hear the word. Treating auditory processing deficits has been made possible through research and advanced training I attended and completed with a psychiatrist Dr. Ron Minson, and his wife Kate Minson. He tells his story about how he found researchers all over the world who discussed their research with him and shared what they knew about listening and language. One of these researchers was Alfred Tomatis, an eye, ear, nose, and throat specialist.

The advanced training was offered in Denver, Colorado for several days giving practitioners time to learn new treatment tools, experience the technology for ourselves, share our own clinical stories of cases we had already treated with this technology, and having the time to ask questions of the whole group of Beta testers that we had become by advancing the settings and types of people we tried the technology on for the first time. The results were also too good to be true, yet the stories proved the outcomes we were all experiencing were happening right before our eyes sometimes instantly and sometimes over the course of weeks depending on the frequency the innovative technology used to treat an individual.

Trust me, I would not be using therapeutic interventions today if they were not safe and if they did not work.

The 50-year-old individual mentioned earlier who had reading comprehension challenges due to Duane's Syndrome, completed the advanced brain training with a recent technology, the Interactive Metronome (IM). It seemed like a miracle that during the training, the individual's eye tracking speed was adjusted and for the first time since birth, the eyes tracking together was more coordinated, corrected through a 6-week IM training program. Now even after two decades, this person reports to still have intact reading and comprehension skills.

Offering this training for most of my healthcare career, I have witnessed and had the opportunity to see and measure the changes in the brain affecting the brain plasticity and how it filled in gaps of sensory processing deficits and unheard-of breakthroughs in so many individuals since the late 1990's. Conferences where clinicians were able to share these types of therapeutic outcomes were so exciting.

From before time, God designed our brains to enjoy all the things that humans possess along with all his creation. We have been given the gift of life and the ability to see in diverse ways, the additional living creation of the lands, seas, and sky beyond where our visual fields reach.

You can be blind yet see with your spiritual eyes beyond the physical world.

The cognitive brain recognizes how and where things are by sight, the size and distance away something is moving by sound, the temperature and hardness of something by touch and feel, and for some who have no sight, they sense via vibration.

The brain receives and analyses information to process responses. Processing feelings of humor was captured clearly in a video I watched and shared with Facebook friends. It featured two toddlers playing with the rubber bands keeping the cabinet door handles closed. Each child took a turn snapping the rubber bands that created uncontrollable laughter. It made me laugh so hard I could not stop watching it. I must have been seeking humor!

Regaining composure is the job of the brain's chemical inhibitors that calm emotions. I must have had to activate those chemicals to an elevated level to calm down the laughter to a calm level before I left the video clip.

Another video I recently watched multiple times, was a mother holding a sleeping swaddled infant in front of a window through which a large gorilla was looking closely at the infant. The adult gorilla responded to what it was observing and launched into the habitat of gorillas to locate and carry an infant gorilla to the window to display its skills playing with the infant mammal.

The difference between HUMANS and the animal kingdom is that God gave us a Soul.

CHAPTER SEVEN

Cognitive Processing

. . . .

There are so many things the brain can do at the same time. The brain is managing your life with and without your awareness. Some functional brain systems happens automatically like your gut, intestines, vital organs, breathing pattern, heart beating speed, initiating your thoughts and actions, controlling your emotional levels, monitoring your reaction to the senses of hearing, seeing, touching, and smelling things internally and externally in your surroundings. We already discussed sleep, pain, sight, and hearing but more complex is how the brain manages it all.

Measuring the situation for safety, or measuring amounts of money, whether you should pick up that piece of furniture, whether you should visit your dying parent all fall to the executive functioning of the brain for making good judgement calls to act on or to let go of. Overeating, over shopping, overindulging in poor choices is sometimes out of balance and the necessary chemicals to inhibit the thoughts or behaviors are missing.

"Think before you speak," and "if you don't have something nice to say… then don't say anything," is something we have all heard over the course of our lifetimes from Parents and Grandparents.

Language in the verbal, visual, written, tactile forms are also functional cognitive parts of brain processing. Reading, hearing, or speaking language involves comprehension of the language. Processing the sequencing and meanings of words is part of reading and listening. Creating pictures in our minds is an essential part of reading and visual memory. Working memory is being able to get through the routine of the day as well as remembering the name of our neighbor and the Grandkids' names. Where we put our mobile and remembering where we parked the car in the parking lot are all part of memory. Recalling that you have an appointment at the hairdresser Saturday is stretching memory over time. Recalling birthdays is part of working memory. Answering philosophical questions involves processing the meaning of words and their uses to explain a concept or to teach someone else about something being able to sequence your thoughts and ideas logically in an organized fashion is a skill of cognitive processing. Sleeping is linked to cognitive functioning.

For some however, like people with genetic conditions, brain injuries from birth or acquired injuries, the ability to control one's emotions, speech, thoughts, verbal, and physical reactions can seem out of balance.

Individuals with deficits in the brain can under react or overreact to internal (inside the body) or external (in the environment) stressors.

Listening is a sensory processing skill. What the person is listening to is where the cognition of the brain takes over. Hearing sounds is a primitive protective sense for safety reasons as are all the other senses. The cognition takes over when it begins to analyze the "what" it has determined that it is hearing, or smelling, or feeling.

"Tag" is a familiar childhood game that sharpens mental/motor responses that help us react fast in harmful situations, like running from a vicious animal, an abusive situation, a fire, a tornado, etc. Another game children might play is, "don't step on the hot lava on the sidewalk" keeping children up on their toes as they work their way through an obstacle course. Games are a wonderful way to exercise our cognitive skills at any age.

Board games and word search games should come off the shelves again to get the kids away from the electronic dangers that are negatively affecting our brains at all ages.

I have a great concern for violent technology that is influencing the future of our existence, the children, teens, young adults, middle aged adults, and some older adults all over the world. The darker the games get the darker our world becomes.

When the unthinkable Columbine school killings happened, and we learned about the backgrounds of the three teens who grew up in decent conditions yet all three seemed to be lacking self-regulation. Did even one of them say to the others, "Guys, I don't think this is a good idea"? is when I began to think about how it was even possible that a game played over and over could influence the brains of descent people to engage in watching and choosing a car, a location, a woman, and the weapon of choice to commit a murder while sportingly in a person's mind and hands, automated of course at first. As the games become less thrilling to the brain and if there is a loss of conscience to override the physical and emotional urges, yes, the loss of one's conscience is clear because there are no consequences when an act of violence is committed. It's only a game that is influencing and overriding natural transmitters of the brain by visual and motor play focusing on the freedom of exploration and content programming of the addictive effects of the game over and over and over and over… to commit murder or other crimes against humanity…has nobody else been draw forward to give warning of such destruction of minds? The military programs in video formatting train defense and offensive moves training for combat in real life situations but have the additional support to guide the career soldier.

I read a study done at a Universities that published a study and reported the benefits of computer-based learning long before Covid isolation, yet I have not seen enough work published that ever made its way to the media platforms to ban these fatal psychological influences. Who is out there addressing the negativity and cons regarding the hours people spend engaged in passively yet powerful brain influencing programs that have already affected the consciences of millions of individuals all over the globe.

One study did report that a larger than expected percentage of men who did not rid their lives of watching porn on their computers, movie screens, or phones by two years passing, were already seeking a thrill beyond their own computer screens and/ or outside of their committed relationship of marriage.

Feeding our brains what they need to survive each day and night is the best remedy for keeping healthy cognitive processing in check.

Reading an enjoyable book snacking on real food sounds good to me right now…

CHAPTER EIGHT

Self-Regulation and Anger Management

Managing your thoughts, emotions, and behavior are all functions of the brain as we have mentioned in past sections of this book.

Self-regulation is the "how" are we managing all these functions? Is a person overly sensitive to what they see, hear, or feel? Are they reacting too fast verbally or physically? Do they know that their voice is louder than the rest of the people in the room?

When they respond, do they respond calmly or in a fit of rage?

When these responses are noticeable, it can be that hearing is off, that defense mechanisms are on high alert, that they are experiencing high pain levels, or they have not been sleeping.

Sometimes rage is the first response rather than having a dimmer switch to engage at a calmer level.

The Interactive Metronome has been successful with individuals who told me they had rage and had undergone anger management classes that had varying results and lasted only a fleeting time.

I met this man at an Interactive Metronome conference, and he was a satisfied participant ready to share his story with me. The man explained that he had remarkable results managing his self-regulation when he went through the IM training program, and he had not had an episode of anger or episodes of rage for over a year since he completed the 6 weeks of training using this IM computer-based tool. This gave me another tool in my toolbox to use with individual's struggling with cognitive, mental, emotional, and behavioral challenges. The benefit of this training works with the brain plasticity, and I have learned so much from my clients. I knew about brain plasticity before it became a word in the neuroscience world. The researcher that gave me the visual evidence that I was seeing success like never before, was Dr. David Amen on a Public TV show talking about the brain. He showed several functional MRIs of brains that had similar patterns. He was able to show the brains of people with ADHD, Parkinson's Disease, Alzheimer's, and many other conditions over additional programs he featured, one being a whole talk about Dementia.

The studies have brought us so much more since his revelation and images of the brains that he discovered and shared with his audiences.

CHAPTER NINE

Timing, Motor Planning, Sequencing, and Motor Coordination

What difference does timing, sequencing, and motor planning make in our lives, anyway?

Timing is at the center of everything our brains and our bodies do. Without timing, sequencing, and motor planning, we would fall, miscalculate stair height, or tip over when riding a bike. Playing sports, reading, speaking, and communicating language whether verbally delivered or written on a piece of paper would be hard without these skills. It could mean the difference between hitting the cymbal too early, right on, or too late for the orchestra conductor's signal to crash the instrument loudly or softly. They say we make a thousand decisions a minute.

Sequencing is putting actions, thoughts, language, and emotion in the right order when speaking, writing, reading, performing on cue, and putting the clothes in the dryer instead of the washer.

Motor planning is what body parts, what direction, how much attention you are going to sequence together to accomplish a task. One unconsciously and consciously moves by carrying out the motor plan taking into consideration how high, how fast, and how hard it is to perform. To walk forward, one must swing the leg from the hip ahead of the opposite foot, land the heel down on the floor, and shift the balance to the forward foot while smoothly rolling onto the toes and stepping down with all your weight onto your heel as you advance forward. After all that, you repeat the same thing with the other leg to create a gait pattern that moves you forward. Your motor plan for walking backwards would be the reverse.

Timing, sequencing, and motor planning together help a person play games, avoid falling, master riding a bicycle, play tennis, drive a car, row a boat, flip pancakes, balance on a skateboard, swim, ski, and even breath. The harder the task, the better timing, sequencing, and motor planning become necessary. We see a high demand for these very skills in competitive sports athletes.

It also matters how one uses tools like eating utensils to get food into the mouth if timing and motor planning are off. Learning to tie shoelaces is a very complex task when children first try to remember the fine motor sequence to make a tight bow. As we age, reaching our feet, losing finger movement, and the sequence patterns will possibly require a change in the style of shoe one can manage to wear, or someone else will need help get them on. The beginning of life is a time of learning and growth. This begins to reverse near the end of a life for us HUMANS. The Golden years of wisdom and grace comes with aging if the loss of mental capacity does not hurry the process.

One may have the sequence pattern to sit down on a toilet, but might lack leg strength, or have knee or back pain, or experience both conditions to get up off the toilet. Sequencing and motor planning how getting into and out of a shower change especially after the surface becomes wet affecting a person's confidence. There are safety devices such as grab bars and tub benches that can be installed in the home to help someone avoid falling and getting injured. These modifications are a common solution and I recommend them in bathrooms if you or someone you know has timing, sequencing, and motor planning with challenges.

Motor Coordination is putting the plan into action from the brain (top down) to the body whether you are holding your breath or blowing out air while swimming, folding clothes, brushing your teeth, doing and exercise routine, playing baseball, driving a moving vehicle, putting the dishes away, scrubbing a bathtub, roller skating, riding a bike, painting your fingernails, changing a diaper, or rocking a baby to sleep. One's movements might be slowing down or impulsively too fast. A person's motor coordination may be efficient and accurate or delayed and not on target. The latter can make things like getting food from a plate into the mouth or like hitting the tennis ball too far out of the court boundaries frustrating. Needing a caregiver to help with eating is a loss and something my clients have experienced grief over. A tennis player can get a coach or use the IM training to get better control of their swing of the racket when their timing and coordination improve. Motor coordination is an essential part of daily living skills.

CHAPTER TEN

Emotion, Anxiety, Perseveration

. . . .

The emotional system is a complex HUMAN feature designed by God to search for Him. When we have anxiety from stress that interferes with sleep because we play reruns in our minds that keep us in a high alert level called perseverative thoughts, we sometimes turn to manufactured substances like sleep meds, watching our TV or our phones, drinking some warm milk or counting sheep.

I recommend talking with God who is waiting for you to tell him what is keeping you awake. He wants to walk you through these worldly interferences, the things that knock you off balance, jam your circadian rhythm, reduce your energy, feeling the pain that keeps gnawing away at you night and day.

Give it all to God. He sent His Son to release you from the worries of sin and darkness. Do not let the enemy who wishes for and seeks out ways that will lead to your demise and down the dark rabbit hole. Tap into the ALMIGHTY, the KING OF KINGS, THE LOVER of all lovers, the Creator, and the Healer, the one who is always by your side. Our bodies are the temple of the Holy Spirit. God lives in your heart, listening to you day and night, waiting to provide special grace to help you to either bear the suffering or to release you from it. Asking for "God's Will to be done," is the ultimate addition to our prayer. That way you are saying that you are willing to endure this trial longer. In any case, you are now a Prayer Warrior because giving God your suffering defeats darkness and opens a way to bring your battle with darkness to the forefront. Whatever it is that is causing you to be depressed rather than overjoyed, is not from God. God did not create evil. Evil created evil by being proud and arrogant against God's perfect Will. Those who say they can do it on their own, thinking of themselves as more like a god who do not think they need help, are kidding themselves.

If you need to speak with a human being along with our Lord's help, God has given gifts to mental healthcare providers. Not all are faith-based believers so you can ask your local Priest or Pastor if they have any recommendations. If not, you can Google 'Christian Psychologist near me.'

I say the Holy Rosary at night before I go to bed. Trust me, I hardly ever make it through the first decade of the Rosary meditating on the first Joyful Mystery, the Annunciation when Mary, who was visited by the Angel Gabriel, announces that she was to become the Mother of God, the Messiah.

Another powerful prayer you can pray is the Chaplet of the Divine Mercy at 3:00 am along with a global team or Prayer Warriors who are following what Jesus said to St. Faustina in the 1930s when He appeared to her and gave her these prayers to say on the Rosary beads along with the request to have His image painted for us to see His victory over our sins by building our faith and washing away our sins with the Blood and Water that gushed forth from His side. His promise to St. Faustina and now to us, is that if anyone says the Chaplet for someone who has died within a day, He will meet the person face-to-face after passing away and give the person one last and final chance to accept Him as their Lord and Savior, the KEY to the GATE of HEAVEN. And by doing that, you may have saved one's poor soul from eternal damnation.

Would that not bring purpose and meaning to your life???

Of course, because you join the ranks of Prayer Warriors for God's armed Warriors.

Bet you will walk your way out of the pit of darkness, depression, and discouragement, right into everlasting life with God in Paradise. There is a mansion waiting for you in Heaven. We can all go with no additional price to pay because death and sin have already been conquered for us. If you acknowledge Jesus as Lord and Savior, that is the key to everlasting life.

I pray we are neighbors when we get there.

I will be praying for all who have read this book and for those who have donated to God's Diamonds foundation committed to feeding the poor and hungry children of the world.

Be BLESSED and be WELL.

Closing Comments

The purpose of this book is to provide a connection between all our HUMANITY and our unique gift of SPIRITUALITY. Humans are complete just the way we are and fully united with our Creator.

Artificial Intelligence is never going to acquire a soul and our virtues of Faith, Long suffering, Hope, Joy, Peace, Patience, Charity/Love that are God-given and the greatest of these is LOVE.

We will not be able to pass our humanity onto manufactured creations no matter how advanced the technology becomes. The movie "1984" was really scarry, for sure. But their computer lacked boundaries and a conscience.

AI technology will never inherit Heaven. AI will have multiple applications that will assist society without our human errors. They will become information highways and faster than our healthcare providers can reach or care for. AI will be able to duplicate our intelligence and this industry may strive to do just that and more successfully.

But God's purpose for us is more powerful as Prayer Warriors doing battle against the darkness that is trying to devalue HUMANITY.

Our identity is recorded in the Book of Life. You will never be just a number.

That dark entity will never succeed in conquering HUMANITY. How do I know… because the Bible tells me so. We all belong to God, and He tells us that nothing can ever separate us from Him. He is holding us by His hand and is our eternal best friend. His presence with us is the most precious and loving relationship we have throughout all of Humanity. SURRENDER TO THIS LOVE that is waiting for your response over and over. Take Christ up on it while you still have time. Jesus spent time in communication with his Father when he became one of us, when he fasted and went to the dessert to pray and speak with his Father. OK…the desert.

If we are true believers and followers… give Jesus a LIKE. Wait a minute… give Him some of your precious time in a quiet state to drink in and soak in and bask in this Golden Eternal LIGHT.

YOU WILL RECEIVE MORE THAN YOU CAN IMAGINE, OR SEE, OR FEEL, OR HEAR, OR TOUCH, OR COGNITIVELY PROCESS, OR DREAM ABOUT.

I just had to tell you some of the things I have learned about HUMANITY and WHAT HUMANS POSSESS.

A young praise group who moves my Spiritual being is Elevation Worship that I ask Alexa to play for me. Amy Grants' early songs do the same thing. Cece Winans is another vocalist I tune in to activate and feed my Spirit.

May God grant you His PEACE and JOY from now to ETERNITY as you live in this vessel called a HUMAN BODY. You are more than that.

It is the best kept secret now unveiled for the world to see.

We are HUMAN and will never lose our power of TRUTH.

THE TRUTH SHALL SET YOU FREE.

BE NOT AFRAID has been stated throughout history.

Remember, the Creator of the Universe loves you, and you have a purpose for being here at this moment in time. Ask God what He wants you to do every day and offer your time and talents to HIM.

Just the other day I asked Jesus if he wanted to help me drive my car and that made me laugh. I heard Jesus laughing too as He placed his spiritual hands over mine on the wheel. He wants to be more present to all of us. Stand up for bringing God into our lives. Pay it forward and feed the hungry.

If you feel moved by the Holy Spirit to do something, then if you feel led to feed hungry children, then donate via our website, GodsDiamonds.net.

We have been feeding children in Detroit, Michigan and in the Philippines. We will be partnering with other foundations as well to strengthen this outreach.

Thank you so much.

Printed in the United States
by Baker & Taylor Publisher Services